# DOES THIS HAPPEN TO EVERYONE?

JAN VON HOLLEBEN

ANTJE HELMS

## A BUDDING ADULT'S GUIDE TO PUBERTY

LITTLe
GeSTALTeN

# CONTENT

# ON GROWING ...

... AND CHANGING

# SWEAT, PIMPLES, HAIR IN NEW PLACES, AND VERY SWEET DREAMS: WHAT TO EXPECT WHEN YOUR HORMONES RUN WILD

# Does Puberty Happen to Everyone?

Yep. Puberty is programmed into all of us. It's part of our genetic material, so everyone goes through it sooner or later, whether they want to or not. When your hormones decide it's time, they send a signal to your brain and the process begins.

Our bodies aren't all on the same schedule, though. It's totally normal for people to start puberty at different times. Also, hormones stay pretty relaxed in some people but go a bit crazy in others. You might find yourself suffering from bad acne, developing big breasts before everyone else, or constantly exploding with anger and bursting into tears. If so, you're either experiencing very strong surges of hormones, or your body is especially sensitive to them. You inherit that from your parents, who almost certainly reacted the same way when they were going through puberty.

Whatever happens, the best thing to do is to stay cool and wait it out. Everything will calm down eventually.

# How Can I Tell If I've Hit Puberty?

You'll sweat more, and your skin and hair will get oily. You'll probably shoot up in height and put on weight. Also, get ready for hair in new places. There's a good reason why we call this part of life puberty: it comes from the Latin word *pubes,* which, as well as meaning "to grow up", can also mean "facial hair" and "pubic hair".

When girls hit puberty, their breasts grow and their hips widen. They will get the first signs of white discharge in their underwear about six months or a year before their period starts. Boys get broader shoulders and their voices break. Both girls and boys will find that their genitals start to grow and change. And if you feel like you're getting a bit chubby, don't worry. Your body needs a lot of energy for all the changes it's going through.

Another thing about puberty is that you'll start to feel differently about your parents. Chances are you'll end up arguing with them more often because you want to run your own life and you're not afraid to say it.

You also might want to be alone a lot. Your body is becoming more important to you and it's normal to want to explore it. Masturbating is a great way of doing that, and it lets you work out what feels good and what doesn't.

And last, but definitely not least: if you haven't got one already, it probably won't be long before you develop your first proper crush.

# Is It Bad If I Haven't Hit Puberty by the Time I'm 13?

Not at all! In fact, if you were alive 150 years ago and you had hit puberty by age 13, you'd have been way, way ahead of all your friends. Back then people's diets weren't as good as they are now, so puberty started much later. Girls didn't usually get their first period until they were about 17 because it took their bodies about that long to reach the 17 percent body fat needed to start their menstrual cycle. It also took boys longer to hit puberty. They started growing later, got body hair later and their voices broke later.

These days we eat better so puberty usually starts earlier. Some girls will actually find that they get their first period around the age of 8. But even if you get to 13 and find you still don't have pubic or underarm hair, you probably have hit puberty—it's just that there are no visible signs of it yet. For a lot of girls, puberty begins in the year leading up to their 10th birthday, which means they're likely to get their first period somewhere between 11 and 13. If your body waits till you're 11 or 12 to kick into gear, then your period will probably start at 13 or 14. Boys can expect their hormones to start running wild sometime between 12 and 15.

But if you still haven't had your first period or ejaculated by the time you are 16, you should talk to your doctor.

# Why Do We Grow Up?
# Why Can't We Stay Kids Forever?

People have different answers to the mystery of why we are born and why we die. Some say it's because of a higher power, while others say that nature or the universe is at the controls. Whatever your beliefs, one thing is for sure: we have to grow up so that we can make new life and keep the cycle of our existence going. If we stayed kids forever and never went through puberty, the human race would die out.

Childhood can seem like a wonderful, carefree time, so it's completely normal to feel sad when you realize that it's coming to an end. When you go through puberty, it's all about change. Your body transforms into something new and your mind starts seeing things differently. It's basically a journey into the unknown and that can feel really scary. But growing up is also exciting. You get to try out new things and you have a whole lot more freedom than you did before. Plus, all the stress and worry that you have to go through to become an adult is actually really useful because it teaches you more about yourself, about other people and about the world.

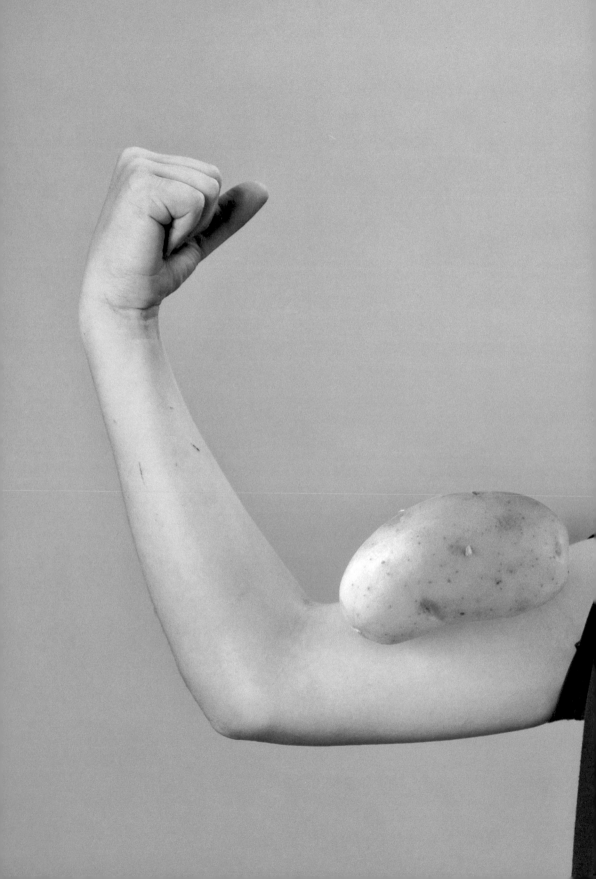

# Do Boys Really Only Think About Cars, Muscles, and Sex?

Well, they do think about them a lot of the time, though it's usually in a different order. Sex is often the number one thing on adolescent boys' minds. For instance, if a girl is speaking to a boy, she might notice that he's just staring at her chest and has zero idea what she's saying. That's because his body is pumped full of testosterone, the male sex hormone that surges during puberty. Muscles are usually number two on the list. For a lot of boys, a hundred push-ups followed by a protein shake is the ideal way to spend their afternoons. Why? Because muscles look good and attract the best partner… or so they say. Those beliefs come from a time way, way back in history when the strongest man would win the best woman. But seeing as our survival no longer depends on hunting and killing wild animals, do boys really need to worry about being super-strong? Funny, charming, sensitive guys who can listen when others talk are often much more attractive (to both sexes) than the ones who spend all of their time working out.

But remember, no two boys think about exactly the same things. They all experience different surges in their hormones during puberty, and they all react to those hormones in different ways.

And another thing: boys aren't the only ones who think a lot about sex. Girls do, too.

# Is It Dangerous to Get a Tattoo or a Piercing?

The first thing you need to know about getting a tattoo is that there are laws in the US about when you can get one, depending on where you live. In some states, you must be 17 or 18 before you can get a tattoo while other states allow you to get one before your 18th birthday as long as you have your parents' permission. It is important that you know what the law is in your state before you get a tattoo and that you only get one somewhere that is licensed and follows those laws to make sure it is safe. The second thing you need to know is that a lot of tattoo inks actually contain the same pigments that are used in car paints. The more colorful the tattoo, the more likely it is that your body won't tolerate it. Your skin might have an allergic reaction and end up itchy or scarred. What's more, the ink (black or colored) can disperse through your body over time and collect in your organs. Many inks also contain chemicals that are known to cause cancer. Some countries have regulations about ingredients that aren't allowed in tattoo ink, but even so, a lot of the other ingredients haven't been tested yet. Basically, there's no real way of knowing what exactly a tattoo will do to your body.

As for piercings, the laws about when and where on your body you can get pierced are much the same as those for getting tattooed and vary state-by-state. Regardless of how old you are when you have it done, piercing can be a risky business. You might end up with an infection or abscess where the needle went in, or you might have an allergic reaction to the metal ring or stud.

Whether your thing is piercing or tattoos, you should think very carefully about whether you really want it and whether you'll still be happy with it in, say, 50 years' time. If you do decide to go for it when you're old enough, make sure that you do your research and ask lots of questions before deciding on a studio. Any reputable studio will be happy to answer your questions and to make sure that safety—yours and theirs—is their number one priority. Since each state has different regulations and local authorities governing studios, it is also a good idea to check with a few different sources to ensure that a studio is reputable. Your local Department of Health will have information on studios in your area, as will the Better Business Bureau. There are also a number of private organizations, like The AAA Tattoo Directory and The Alliance of Professional Tattooists, Inc., that are dedicated to health and safety issues of body art and can provide lists of approved studios in your area.

# Why Do Girls Get Breasts
# but Boys Don't?

Because the Y chromosome, which is what decides that a fertilized egg will grow into a baby boy, doesn't carry any blueprints for breasts. Men still have nipples, of course, but they don't actually serve any purpose. They're just part of the basic package that all of us are made of and they begin to form a few weeks after sperm meets egg. Girls develop breasts so that, later on in life, they can feed their babies if they have them.

Boys can actually sometimes get sort of breasts. About 50 percent of boys find that when they hit puberty the area around their nipples swells and stays like that for a while. In most cases the swelling goes down on its own.


# Why Are Some Girls so Touchy
# Before Their Period?

They don't do it on purpose—it's out of their control. See, a few days before a girl gets her period, her hormone levels plummet. Really fast. That might make her feel rotten and as if she's the most unpopular person in the world. She may be easily offended and irritable. She might even be aggressive and do or say hurtful things. Plus, she'll be just as shocked at what her alter ego is up to as you are. But, girls? As unpleasant as this PMS (premenstrual syndrome) can be, it's not a get-out-of-jail-free card that lets you behave as badly as you like. So if your Mrs Hyde makes you step too far out of line, make sure you apologize ASAP.

Herbal remedies like St John's Wort and Agnus Castus can help relieve the symptoms of PMS. As with any medications, even herbal remedies, make sure to check with your doctor before you take them.

# What Can I Do About My Acne?

So there's this boy standing in front of the mirror and examining his face.

Boy: Mom, Mom! I've stopped getting pimples!

Mom: How did you manage that?

Boy: There's no room left.

All right, we can joke all we want, but everyone knows acne isn't funny. Unfortunately, it's often a big part of puberty, so if you want to know how to tackle it, read on.

Boys tend to get more acne than girls during puberty because they have more of the male sex hormone testosterone swimming around in their blood. Testosterone makes the sebaceous glands start producing an oily substance called sebum, which, when mixed with dead skin cells, can clog up pores and lead to blackheads and pimples. Squeezing your pimples (tempting as it is) usually only makes things worse because it just loads the pores up with more dirt. The best thing to do is wash your face twice a day with warm water and a gentle soap or cleanser. If you have a lot of pimples, speak to your pharmacist about treatments containing salicylic acid. Concealer is quite good at hiding pimples, but like all makeup it also clogs up your pores. If you suffer from severe acne, your doctor can refer you to a dermatologist.

Your sebaceous glands aren't the only ones to kick into gear during puberty. The sweat glands in your armpits, around your genitals and on your feet also start working. And, okay, we might be descended from animals, but we've come a long way since then. Male capuchin monkeys attract females by washing in their own pee, and we probably all agree that we're not into that, right? So, showering or washing every day is the way to go. Genitals just need water, or a mild soap if you feel it's necessary. Girls, just wash your vulva (don't wash inside your vagina) and go from front to back. Boys, if you are circumcised, gently wash your entire pubic area daily with mild soap and water. If you are uncircumcised, gently pull back your foreskin to wash off the secretions that collect under there. But only do this if it's easy. If pulling back the skin hurts because it's too tight, make an appointment with your doctor.

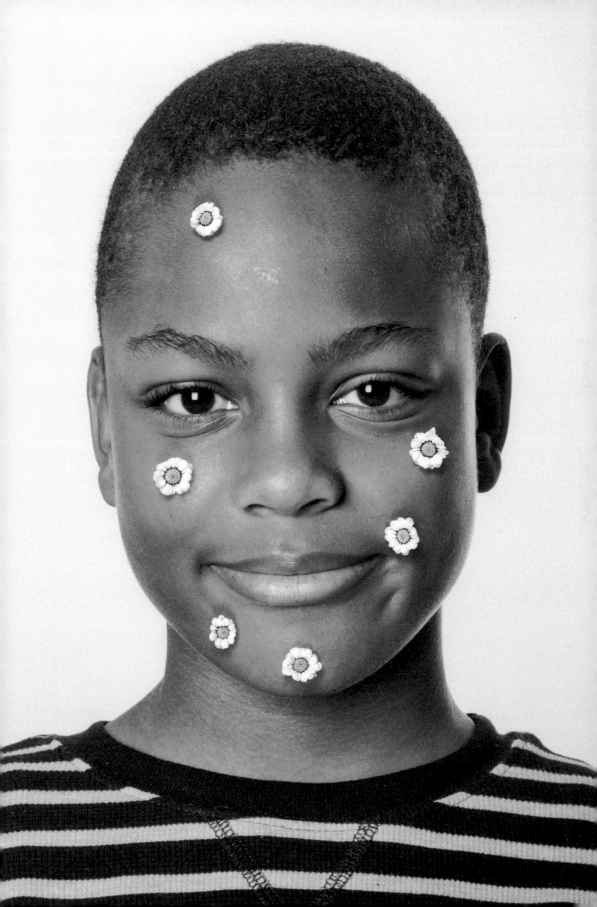

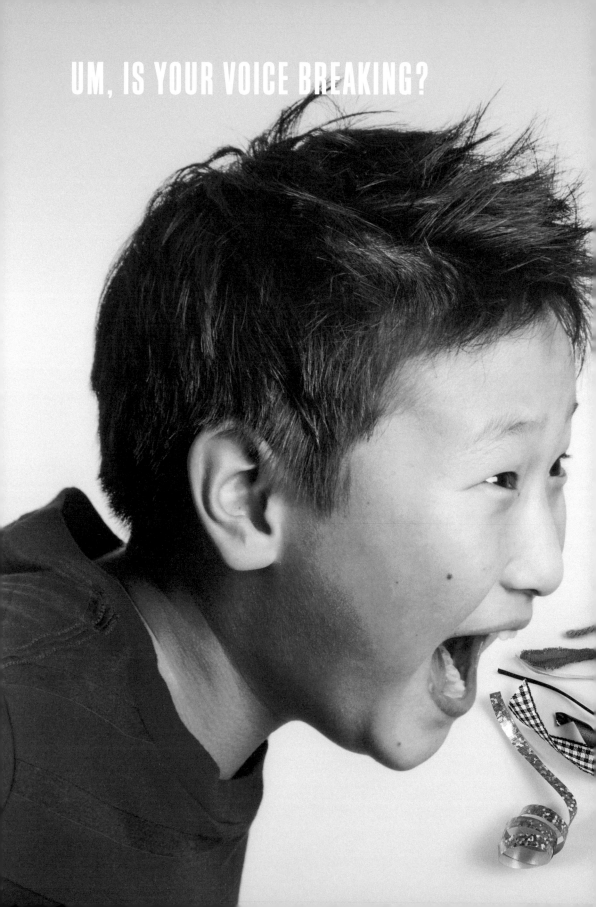

UM, IS YOUR VOICE BREAKING?

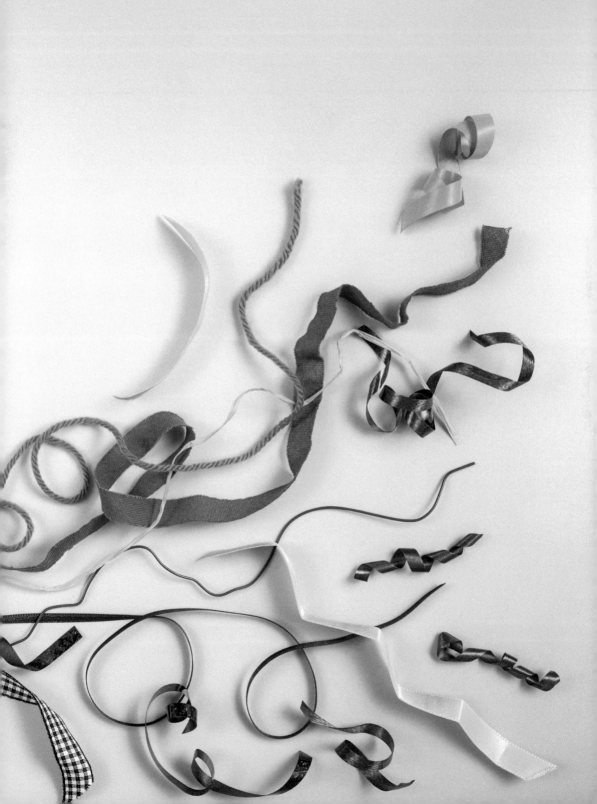

# Is It Only Boys' Voices That Break?

When a boy's voice starts yo-yoing between high, low, squeaky, and scratchy, then you can be pretty sure his voice is breaking. It can take between nine months and two years for his voice to work out where it belongs (usually around an octave lower). By the time boys are 15, their voice box and vocal chords are usually fully grown and they have to switch from the boys' choir to the men's. On an interesting side note, things were very different 250 years ago when composer Joseph Haydn was still singing with the Vienna Boys' Choir at 18.

Girls don't escape this change altogether. Their voices usually drop by about a third, but unlike with boys, you can't usually tell it's happening.

# Why Are Some Boys so Short and Others Practically Giants?

Because the speed at which hormones trigger changes during puberty differs from person to person. A boy might shoot up overnight when he hits 14, but some of his friends might already have done it, and others might still be waiting. Once they start though, boys can grow by as much as four inches a year. Often their hands, feet, arms and legs will go first, which is why some boys look a bit beanpole-ish for a while. The rest of their body will catch up eventually and their proportions will even out, but they might have to wait till their early 20s for that to happen.

# Why Do We Have Pubic Hair?

"Hey there, gorgeous. Check me out, all sexually mature. My pubic hair smells so good it's making me totally irresistible, am I right?!" That, in case you were wondering, is what a male gorilla would say to his mate if he was in the habit of thinking about his brand-new hair-down-there. He'd never dream of trimming it or shaving it all off, though. That's because, for many animals, pubic hair gives off a scent designed to attract the opposite sex. We humans also find ourselves attracted to other people because of the unique way they smell, and a bit of hair makes it all the easier to sniff out.

# I Used To Think Girls Were Stupid. Why Do I Suddenly Like Them Now?

Remember how you used to play superheroes in the playground? How you and the rest of the boys would all run around shouting and pretending to shoot each other? You probably thought there was no room for stupid girls in a game like that. Plus, they didn't even want to play. Why? Because they were all about being girls back then, and you were all about being boys. When kids are younger, they have to work out their identity and gender roles. To do so, boys and girls often separate off from each other in grade school and behave in ways that overemphasize their girlishness or boyishness. Sometimes it can go as far as both sides being nasty to each other just to make themselves feel better. Once you hit puberty, though, you've sorted out all your differences and suddenly opposites start to look very attractive indeed. But opposite doesn't necessarily mean someone of the opposite sex. A boy might get a crush on a boy, or a girl might start fancying another girl. Maybe you're fascinated by how different the other person is, or maybe you find them interesting because they're so similar to you.

# Is It Bad to Start Shaving When You're 11 or 12?

Why should it be bad? It's your body and you get to decide whether you want it with hair or without. Body hair is a sign that you're growing up, and being grown-up means learning to make your own decisions. Do you hate the way your facial hair hasn't started growing evenly yet? Then get rid of it! Can't be bothered to shave your legs or under your arms? Then leave them be!

If you decide to shave, make sure that it's because you don't like your hair. Don't just do it because everyone else is, or because you think you should. Some people are big fans of their body hair because it makes them feel older. Also, whatever anyone might say, there's nothing unhygienic about pubic hair. Thoughts on hair are different all over the world. Did you know that a lot of young women in Japan actually wear pubic wigs? They do it because they don't tend to have much hair themselves and in their country having thick pubic hair is considered especially feminine and a healthy sign of fertility.

In short, what you do with your hair—facial, pubic, underarm, leg—is up to you, and you alone. Try shaving it, try letting it grow. Make sure you use a good razor with a protective coating, and remember that the skin around your pubic area will be really sensitive.

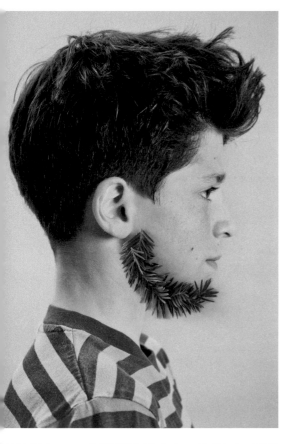
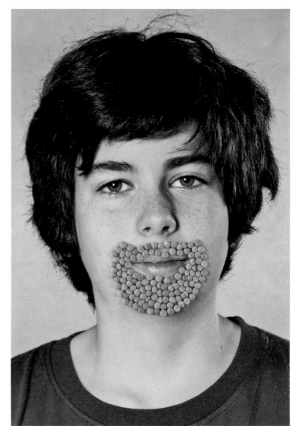

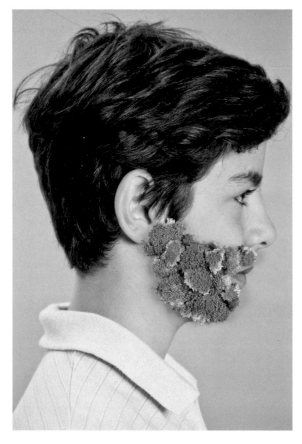
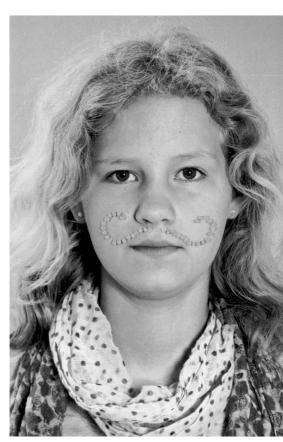

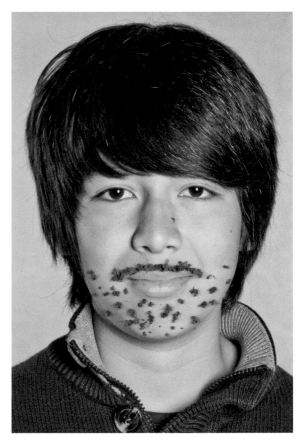

# ON BEING A GIRL ...

... AND BEING A BOY

# TOO BIG, TOO SMALL, TOO LONG, TOO SHORT: WHY YOU'RE OKAY EXACTLY THE WAY YOU ARE

## Is There Anything I Can Do or Eat to Make My Breasts Grow?

There's nothing you can do to change the breasts your body has in store. In this department, like so many others, every woman is unique. Some breasts are big, some are small, some are oval like a pear or round like an apple, and some hang low while others stay high.

When you hit puberty, the female sex hormone estrogen gives the signal for your breasts to start growing. You might find that your left breast grows first, then the right catches up. Or vice versa. Everything ends up pretty well balanced after a while, although very few women have two breasts that are exactly the same size. If your breasts start growing early, they'll probably stop growing fairly quickly. But if they put in an appearance later, they'll need a bit longer to finish growing. Some girls are 21 before their breasts get to where they need to be. And when it comes to boyfriends or girlfriends, the size or shape of your breasts is really not important. What matters is the whole you—your personality, your charisma, and a big helping of self-confidence that says, "Hey, this is me. This is my body and I think it's pretty great just the way it is."

# NO TWO PEARS ALIKE

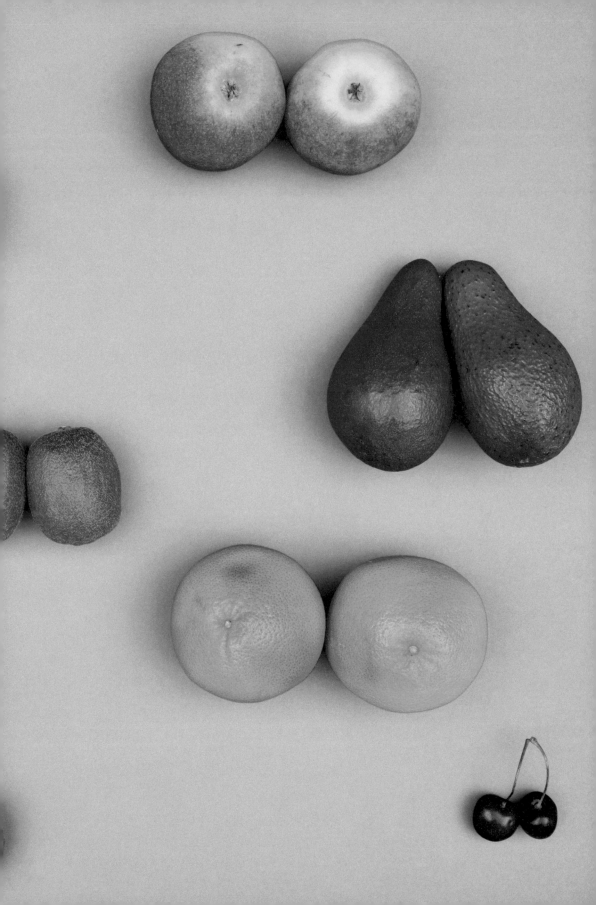

# What Does the Inside of a Breast Look Like?

The inner workings of a breast are fascinating. Alongside nerves, veins, and things called lymphatic vessels, there's also a whole network of mammary glands and milk ducts, all cushioned in protective fatty tissue. The mammary glands are usually so small that you can't feel them. Only when a woman gets pregnant, and especially when the baby arrives and she starts breastfeeding, do they become fully developed. If you're thinking that small breasts might make it hard to feed a baby, don't worry. The size of your bra has nothing to do with your ability to breastfeed.

You might well find that your breasts sometimes feel swollen and a bit sore. This often happens before your period and it's completely normal. The monthly ups and downs of your hormones are to blame, and everything should settle down again once your period finishes.

# Cookie, Vajayjay, Lady Bits: What Is Your Vagina All About?

Ever heard of the word vulva? Sounds kind of nice, don't you think? It comes from Latin and refers to the area that includes the clitoris, labia and the opening to the vagina (the tube that leads from the vulva to the cervix). If someone talks about their "lady bits" they usually mean both the vulva and the vagina. It's entirely up to you whether you want to say vulva, coochie, vag, or anything else that sounds good to you. You could even think up your own name for it if you like. Something that sounds nice to you. We mostly use vulva in this book, because it's often the most suitable and up-to-date way of talking about this part of the body.

# How Often Will I Get My Period?

With most women it happens once a month, usually around the same date every time. As soon as your body has worked out its rhythm, you'll find it gets quite easy to predict when your next period is going to be.

The average menstrual cycle lasts about 28 days. You start bleeding on Day one, when your uterus expels the lining it built up for a fertilized egg that never appeared. Women generally find that they bleed for somewhere between three and seven days. Around the end of the first week of your cycle the sex hormone estrogen tells your uterus to start building up another lining. Your body produces a lot of estrogen in the middle of the cycle so that one of your ovaries releases an egg that travels into the fallopian tube. Once that happens, another hormone, progesterone, makes the lining of the uterus get really thick so it will be a comfortable home for a fertilized egg. However, if an egg doesn't embed itself in the lining during the second half of the cycle, your hormone levels will fall and you'll get your next period. The actual length of the cycle varies from woman to woman, and can be anywhere between 20 and 35 days.

It's completely fine if your periods don't come regularly at first. Some girls find it takes quite a long time before everything settles down.

# Can You Bleed to Death Because of Your Period?

No, don't worry. You have over four quarts of blood in your body, and most women only lose between four and 12 tablespoons during their period. That's less than one ounce, and three-quarters of it usually goes in the first three days. Also, there's nothing wrong with you if you feel tired and run down during your period. Most women do. You can pep yourself up by relaxing for a while, or by doing the exact opposite. Exercising and focusing your mind on something else often helps to soothe period pain.

Some cultures hold a celebration when a girl gets her period for the first time. After all, being able to create new life and bring it into the world is really nothing short of a miracle. So why not do something special when you get your first period? You could organize your own private party, say. If you like the idea, think about it and decide what you want to do. But if you'd rather not mark the occasion, then that's totally fine, too.

# REALLY? IS THAT ALL?

# Do Tampons Hurt?

Tampons? Nope. Totally harmless. As long as a tampon is positioned right, it won't hurt or feel like it's poking you. In fact, you won't even know it's there. The only time inserting a tampon might cause you discomfort is if your vagina is a bit dry, like at the start or end of your period, when it might chafe a little. You don't need to worry about your hymen either. It's stretchy and actually only covers part of the vaginal opening—how else would your body be able to get rid of blood during your period?

When you're ready to try out a tampon, make sure you choose a time when you won't have to rush. It's best to start out with the smallest size, and it's up to you whether you choose the kind you insert with your finger or the kind that comes with a special applicator. Read the instructions inside the package carefully. Also, you should never use tampons when you're not on your period. Panty liners are the way to go if you want protection from normal discharge.

Tampons aren't the only option that you have when you're on your period. You can also use maxi-pads, which are absorbent pads that stick to the inside of your underwear. You can also use menstrual cups, which are small cups made of a special kind of silicon that you can use again and again. You insert them into your vagina like a tampon, but they collect the blood instead of absorbing it.

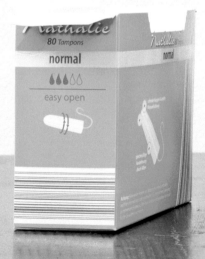

Nathalie
80 Tampons
normal
easy open

**EVERYONE IS UNIQUE**

# How Big Should a Penis Be?

A penis is an amazing thing. A master of disguise, you could say. One that looks small when it's just hanging around might grow really big when it's erect, and one that's already pretty big when flaccid might not change much when it gets hard. So what about yours? When it comes to length, it might well be within the average for the United States, where the typical penis measures around five and a half inches when erect. Your penis will begin to grow just after you hit puberty, and usually only stops once it's all over. The same goes for your testicles, which are responsible for producing the male sex hormone testosterone.

Penises can be big, small, long, short, fat, thin, or curved, and your genes decide what yours will look like. No two penises are the same, which makes sense, right? After all, it's not as if your nose is the spitting image of everyone else's. Differences are what make life interesting. And in case you were wondering, the length or width of a penis is almost never important when it comes to having sex.

# When Will I Start Producing Sperm?

It's all up to your genes. They've got the timetable that says when you'll start producing sperm and when you'll ejaculate semen for the first time. Most boys find this happens between 11 and 15, when their testosterone levels are high enough. It's very common for boys to ejaculate for the first time in their sleep. If you wake up and find that your boxers or sheets are a bit sticky, it means you were probably having an especially nice dream last night. Ever heard someone mention a wet dream? Well, this is it. Also, if you find that no liquid comes out when you masturbate, don't worry. It soon will.

# Why Are Some Boys Circumcised?

Circumcision is a cultural norm in many places in the world, including the United States. Most baby boys, about 75 percent in the US, are circumcised shortly after birth, either at the hospital or in a separate religious ceremony. The practice is also a traditional part of some religions, such as Judaism and Islam.

The foreskin is a hood of skin that protects the sensitive head of a boy's penis, known as the glans. If you are not circumcised when you are a baby, occasionally the foreskin can become too tight as you grow and it won't slide back when the penis is erect. This can cause a great deal of pain and make it difficult to urinate. The problem often sorts itself out during puberty, but if it doesn't, circumcision is one of the options available. This is a straightforward operation that often just removes part of the foreskin. As a nonsurgical solution, stretching exercises using special creams can help relieve the problem.

# What Is Semen Made Of?

Mostly fructose and a kind of high-performance lubricant. Only a very small percentage of semen is made up of sperm, the tiny cells that contain our DNA and have long tails that propel them forwards really quickly. The rest is a mixture of different kinds of substances. A high-fructose fluid secreted by the seminal vesicles gives the sperm the energy they need, while the prostate produces a substance that makes them strong and keeps them mobile. A healthy man will have between 20 million and 150 million sperm in just a quarter teaspoon of semen. He will release an average of one-half to one and a half teaspoons of semen when he ejaculates, which adds up to about 900 million sperm at most (it won't be so many when you're just starting puberty, though).

Now, 900 million sperm might sound like a lot, but try telling that to the southern right whale. All you'll get is a weary smile as he explains that his testicles each weigh over 1100 pounds and can produce over five gallons of semen.

But back to us humans. Semen doesn't always have the same consistency. It can change from milky to translucent to thick and stringy. Ejaculate several times in a row, and you'll find that your semen gets clearer because it has fewer sperm in it. And if you happen to have a microscope at home, you could put it to good use and check out the wriggling little tadpoles for yourself.

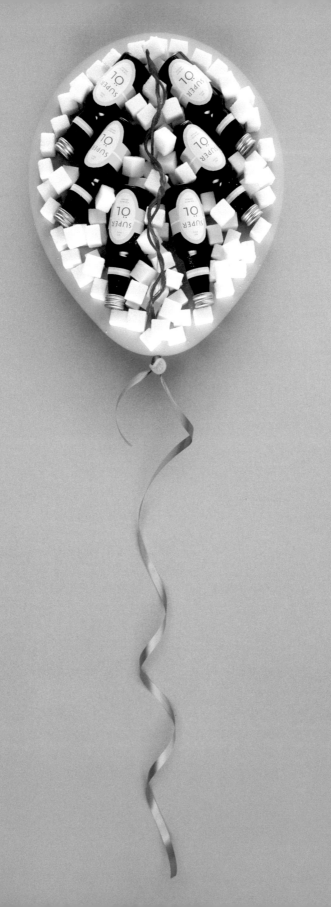

BOY OR GIRL?

# ON CRUSHES AND
# FALLING IN LOVE

# BEATING HEART, BUTTERFLIES, TINGLING ALL OVER, AND WHERE DID MY APPETITE GO? WHAT LOVE IS AND HOW IT MAKES YOU FEEL

## How Do You Write a Love Letter?

Take some time and think about why you like this person so much. What is it about him that you find so attractive? Why does she make you happy and what are the things about his personality that you think are really great? How do you feel when you're close to her? Do you love his eyes? Her smile? Is it the similarities you share that make you feel good all over? Is there anything that you're scared of? Once you've thought about all those things, then start writing. Just let the words appear on the page exactly the way they come into your head. If you do that, the letter will express the real you. That's important because a love letter is about helping the other person discover something new about you. But don't ask them to do anything. If you do, it will make them feel under pressure and no one enjoys feeling like that. Also, don't just copy any ready-made texts from the internet. You want your letter to be specific to you two, not to a gazillion other people you've never met.

A lot of people like to get nice messages on Facebook, too. And texting the guy or girl of your dreams (maybe with a cute smile) to tell them that you're thinking of them might really make their day.

# How Do You Find the Right Girl for You?

Wow, that's a tricky question. It's really hard to know whether someone is right for you or not. Some people have a long list of what they want in a girlfriend or boyfriend—outgoing, funny, sensitive, good-looking—but no one is going to be able to check all the boxes, so setting out with a checklist isn't a good way to get the girl. What happens most of the time is that you fall for someone when you least expect it. Plus, that person is often completely different from the one you thought you wanted.

Just keep your eyes open. Maybe the girl of your dreams takes the same route to school as you. Or it might be someone you've known for ages, someone who likes the same things as you, or someone who's into hobbies you've never tried. And be brave! If there's a girl you like, go up to her—at school, at a party, in town or after sports practice—and invite her out on a date. You'll probably know within a few seconds if it's likely to work out or not.

We often have to experience a few different people before we find someone we want to stay with. Hopping into bed with each other right at the start is a bad idea because it feels horrible if you realize afterwards that the person wasn't right for you.

# Is It True That Boys Act All Weird When They Like a Girl?

Having a crush on someone, whether it's a boy or a girl, is a completely new experience for kids going through puberty. It's exciting and scary all at once. If a boy gets a crush on a girl, he might worry a lot about things like not being liked by the girl of his dreams or about his friends making fun of him.

The more uncertain a boy is about how he should behave, the weirder he can act. He might spend the whole time messing around, show off much more than usual, or even give you the cold shoulder. The last thing he wants to do is come across as being gentle or vulnerable. But in actual fact, a sensitive guy can be really attractive. Macho types are often a lot less interesting than boys who are genuine and not afraid to admit what they are feeling.

# What Is Love?

Love is thinking about someone all day and then dreaming about them at night. Love is sending each other a million text messages, and then turning your phones off when you're together. But hang on, isn't that how you feel when you have a crush? Butterflies going crazy in your stomach, heart beating so fast it's hard to breathe, the fear of making a fool of yourself at the very moment you have to be at your most spectacular? Everything looks incredible and exciting because you're seeing the world through the rose-tinted glasses that your hormones made especially for this occasion.

Liking someone, having a crush on them, can feel intoxicating and is often the first step on the path to falling in love. But not every crush has to end in love. Sometimes you fall for someone and then realize pretty quickly that they're not really right for you after all. When you've seen the other person's weaknesses, when you sometimes even get annoyed with them but still really want them in your life, then you can start talking about love. Sex can be a way of expressing that feeling, which is why people often call it making love.

You can also have love without sex. It's called platonic love, and it's the way you feel about people like your friends, parents, brothers, or sisters.

# What Do I Do If a Girl Likes Me, but I Don't Feel the Same Way?

The best, fairest way to deal with it is to talk to her. If you decide to ignore her, she might find you even more attractive or you might end up hurting her. Whatever you do, don't make fun of her feelings or talk about them behind her back with your friends. Would you like it if someone did that to you? Pick a time when the two of you are alone and say something like "Hey, I feel like you've got a crush on me. The thing is, I don't feel the same way. I don't want to hurt you, but please don't think that anything's going to happen between us." If you do that, she'll see that you respect her and will know where she stands.

# Can You Stop Yourself from Loving Someone?

Even though it can really hurt, it's best to let yourself feel things like sadness, anger, and disappointment. If you've been dumped, you'll probably feel like crying the whole time. That's okay. It's all part of the process. Go to your friends, siblings, or parents for support. Talk about your feelings or write them down. Try and take your mind off things by doing things you enjoy like watching movies or playing sports.

All those suggestions are much better ways of getting over someone than trying to convince yourself that your ex was stupid and you never liked them anyway. Over time, your love for them will fade and you'll find that you're ready for someone new.

# How Do I Know if I've Fallen for Someone?

Inside, you feel like running around, shouting Yeeeaaah! at the top of your lungs. It puts you in the best mood ever and nothing can ruin it. You're a step away from being able to fly and you'd just love to give the whole world a big fat bear hug. Outside, though, it might be that the moment your crush gets close, you freeze up like a deer in headlights and can barely make a noise, let alone speak or move. Or you might be so keen to impress the other person that you go totally crazy, acting the clown and losing all ability to sit still. Oh, and be prepared for everything (friends, family, school, hobbies) to evaporate from your mind as you spend every waking moment trying to work out when you'll next get to see the girl or boy who has captured your heart.

# How Can I Persuade a Boy to Like Me?

Sorry to be the bearers of bad news, but there's no magic potion that will convince someone to fall in love with you. What you can do, though, is show him that you like him. That's the first step. Be interested in what he has to say, ask him what kind of music he likes, and maybe suggest going to a movie together. Tell him about yourself and what kind of things you like—that's a good way of bringing the two of you closer. But don't go over the top, and definitely don't suck up to him. That kind of thing only works between animals. Take chimpanzees, for example. If a male shares his food with a female, she rewards him with sex. Acting like that, whether you're a girl who likes a boy or a boy who likes a boy, is definitely not a road you want to go down.

You'll notice soon enough if your crush likes you back. If he's clearly not interested in you, then step away. You can't force these things. But even though you never know the outcome at the start, dare to take a risk and make your feelings clear. Being rejected is not half as painful as never having the courage to try.

# Is it Possible to Love More Than One Person at the Same Time?

Yes. You've got a big heart and there's room for a lot of people in there. It's normal to have lots of friends who you like for different reasons and hang out with at different times. It's also possible to have romantic feelings for more than one person and to find it hard to decide who you like most. You might not even want to decide. But after a while you'll probably find that your feelings for one person are stronger than for all the others. If that doesn't happen, then you need to be open and honest with everyone involved. Respect their feelings and treat them fairly. Jealousy can be a big problem in these situations, as most people don't like the idea of their girlfriend or boyfriend being interested in anyone else.

# What Do You Have to Do When You Have a Boyfriend or Girlfriend?

You probably have to do chores at home, and you definitely have to do your homework, but when it comes to a loving relationship, you shouldn't have to do anything. Whatever the two of you do together must only happen because both of you want it to. Neither one of you should force the other into doing anything, especially when it comes to sex. This is teamwork, and both of you need to be on board. Listen to what your body is telling you and trust your gut instinct. If you're not ready for French kissing or sex, then that's totally fine. The only person who gets to decide what you do with your body is you.

Having said that, a few tips can be helpful when you're in a relationship. First, be honest. Don't expect the other person to be a mind reader. Don't be clingy. Listen. Tell the other person what you want instead of complaining that you're not getting it. And don't expect too much. No one can do everything you want them to do, have everything you want them to have, and know everything you want them to know!

# ON KISSING ...

... AND SEX

# MAKING OUT AND MAKING IT ... OH YEAH: WHAT, WHEN, WHERE, WHY, WHO WITH, AND HOW TO PROTECT YOURSELF

## How Do You Kiss?

Don't ask us—go and try it out for yourself! Have fun, and don't take your first few kisses too seriously. For most boys and girls, being able to laugh with each other as you work things out is a really important part of learning to kiss. Plus, laughter is relaxing and a kiss feels much nicer if your mouth isn't all tense.

No two kisses are the same. They can last for a long time or be short and super-sweet. They can be wet, dry, or nibbly, wild and passionate or soft and shy. You might feel like closing your eyes one time and keeping them open another. But what every kiss has in common is that they cause your body to release happiness hormones known as endorphins. In other words, kissing makes you feel goooood.

Still, we're not sure how happy the Thai couple felt when they broke the world record for the longest kiss in 2012. They made out for a full 50 hours! Doesn't just reading that make your jaw ache?

# How Old Do You Have to Be to Start Kissing?

Are you ready? You're sure? Then smooch away! Unlike with sex, there's no minimum age for kissing. Just make sure that you feel comfortable with the other person and that no one is forcing you to kiss them against your will. Some countries have strict rules about kissing, though, so watch out if you get a crush on someone while you're on vacation or if you move. Some of the more conservative states in the US, for instance, have rules that stop kids kissing in school.

# What Is Sex?

We're not Komodo dragons, head lice or earthworms. They can all reproduce without partners, but if humans don't have sex with each other, there would soon be none of us left. That's why nature has given us a sex drive, which means that most of us want to have sex and enjoy doing it. After all, it'd be pretty stupid if we had to keep our species going by doing something that didn't feel good, right?

Even if someone doesn't want children, they will probably still want to have sex. On the other hand, people can have sex but still be unable to have a baby. That's the case with homosexual couples and with some heterosexual couples. In those situations, people often use artificial insemination or adoption if they want to start a family.

Sex is also a way to express your love for someone, and it can be lots of fun. When two people have sex, it's their way of saying: "I think you're the greatest and I want to share this experience with you". And you know what? Sex isn't just about intercourse; it's also about kissing, stroking, massaging. In fact, sex is anything that turns you on, which means everyone is free to decide what sex means for them.

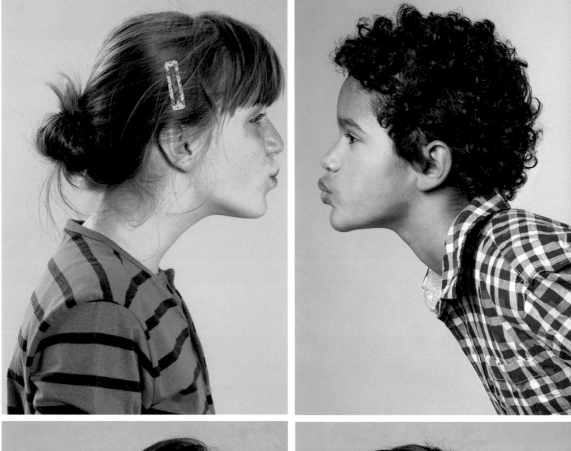
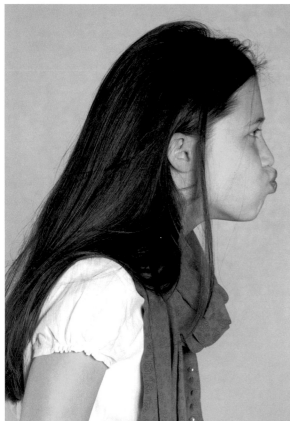
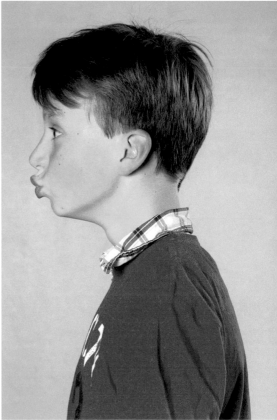

# How Old Do You Have to Be Before You Can Have Sex?

The age of consent for homosexual and heterosexual sex in the United States differs in each state. Most states set the limit between 16 and 18 years of age, but it can also depend on how old your partner is and what type of relationship you have with them, for instance if you are close in age or married. Lawmakers decided on this limit because they believe that, at the age of consent, you are old enough to take responsibility for yourself and for your body. Reaching that level of maturity isn't just about having sex, though; it also means being able to work out whether this or that person is someone you want to have sex with, and having the confidence to say "no" to sex. Not everyone feels able to do all that when they're 16, 18, or even older. It's up to you to work out whether you're ready or not.

If you have sex under the age of consent in your state, there is a chance that your partner could face criminal charges and those charges could be serious. For example, in some states, like California, it is a crime called statutory rape for anyone older than 18 to have sex with anyone under the age of 18 and it can carry a punishment of jail time and having to register as a sex offender. However, in other states, like Indiana, if you are between 16 and 18 years old and your partner is older than 18, but close in age to you, it is not a crime as long as you both want to have sex with each other and there is no sign of abuse or exploitation. The laws about age of consent can be a little confusing, so if you are thinking of having sex with someone who is older than you are, you can always check with your state's Department of Health and Human Services or even a local chapter of Planned Parenthood to find out what is legal and what is not in your area.

But even once you are legally old enough for sex, there is still a danger that someone older than you might try to persuade you to have sex against your will. If an adult in a position of trust (this might be a teacher or your sports coach) gets you to have sex with them before you're 18 by, for example, promising you better grades or a better position on the team, you will feel used and maybe even abused afterwards.

One more thing—even though you're legally allowed to have sex at at a certain age, studies show that a lot of people wait longer than the age of consent before they lose their virginity. Take your time. There's no rush. It's a very personal decision and you're the one who gets to decide, together with the person you want to sleep with, when the time is right.

# How Long Does Sex Last?

Most men ejaculate about three minutes after penetration. That might not sound like long, but intercourse is just one part of sex and there are lots of ways to extend those three minutes. You could take a break from intercourse to try out something different on each other for a bit, and then go back to what you were doing. If you both relax and have fun, sex can sometimes last for hours and yet feel like mere seconds.

Basically, time isn't all that important here. Just enjoy exploring each other's bodies and discovering what feels good for you both. A lot of people find that, even though they enjoy having sex and reaching orgasm, being intimate with their partner is actually the most important part of the equation.

# Can My Parents Forbid Me from Having Sex?

Not really. However, they make the rules in your house so they can forbid you from having sex there. If they know that you are having (or going to have) sex, they are perfectly within their rights to advise you against it. That might make you angry, but you never know, maybe their reasons aren't as stupid as they first seem. Perhaps you've been letting your schoolwork, friends, and everything else slide since you started having sex with your boyfriend or girlfriend? In that case, it's understandable that they're worried about you and want to stop you from throwing your life away. If your parents are really concerned about your relationship (say your partner is much older than you), then they can get in touch with social services, who would then decide how to deal with the situation.

Then again, maybe you're fine and they're worrying for nothing. Remember, it might be hard for your parents to deal with the idea of you having sex, and they probably just want to protect you and stop you from getting hurt. The best thing to do is talk to them about it.

# Is Sex Dangerous or Unhealthy?

Sex can be one of the healthiest things in the world. When you sleep with someone, in fact even when you just start kissing and touching, your body releases endorphins, which are hormones that boost your immune system and make you feel happy. Things that have nothing to do with sex, like laughing, passing an exam or, exercising, will also get the endorphins flowing. But, the feel-good factor with sex only applies if you are sleeping with someone because you want to. Being forced to have sex against your will is frightening and can put your mental health at risk.

You also need to be aware of sexually transmitted infections (STIs). These are bacterial or viral infections that are transmitted between people when they have sex. Being in love with someone and trusting them doesn't mean that you are protected from STIs. The best way to avoid catching one is to use a condom every time you have sex. The more often you have unprotected sex, the more likely you are to become infected with a virus or bacteria that can cause pain and even effect your ability to have babies in the future. You will also be in danger of contracting HIV/AIDS, which is an STI that can kill you.

# How Old Do I Have to Be Before I Can Get the Pill Without My Parents' Consent?

No matter what the age of consent is where you live, you can get contraception (including the pill) at any age and without your parents knowing. That means the doctor or nurse who you speak to cannot force you to tell your parents, although he or she might encourage you to do so. Also, doctors and nurses will only prescribe the pill if they believe that you fully understand all the information you are given and the decision you are making. If they have good reason to believe you are at risk (e.g. from abuse), they will consider telling someone. This will only happen if the risk is serious, and they would probably talk to you first.

It's important to know two things about the pill: a) you don't have to go on it, and b) it protects against pregnancy but not STIs. Using a condom is the only way to keep from getting pregnant and you or your partner from getting an STI. As long as you use it properly, a condom is a very effective method of contraception. Plus, you don't have to swallow any hormones for it to work. You can buy condoms at any age, and they're available from all sorts of places, including supermarkets, pharmacies, and delis. Also, they're a lot easier to use than you might think.

The only time it might be okay not to use a condom is if you are taking another form of contraception and you both trust each other enough to know for sure that there is no danger of either of you catching anything. If you are worried about HIV/AIDS, you can visit your local Planned Parenthood clinic for a free and confidential test. You don't have to give your real name, and the result will not appear on any of your records.

# How Safe Are Condoms?

If used properly, condoms are 98 percent effective at protecting against pregnancy and STIs. The pill is even better at preventing pregnancy but does not stop you from getting STIs.

When handling a condom, make sure it doesn't catch on your fingernails. Don't leave it lying in the sun, and don't keep one in your wallet for ages. If you've had one for a while, check its use-by date. Avoid Vaseline, oil-based lubricants, and massage oils, as these will all damage the latex that condoms are made of. It's a good idea to read the instructions in the package and practice a few times before you actually need to use one. Also, condoms come in different sizes. Because your penis is still growing during puberty, there's a good chance that standard condoms, which are about two inches wide, will be a bit too big. That's a problem as it might slip off during sex. You can get narrower (and wider) condoms online, from your pharmacist, or from specialty shops.

# What Are You Supposed to Think About When You're Having Sex?

The great thing about sex is that it can make all the thoughts fly right out of your head. When two people sleep together, it's not unusual for them to feel completely fulfilled and to only have space in their heads for each other and the sex that they're having.

So, you might have loads of homework to do, a mountain of chores to get

through, a major tennis tournament to win, and the party of the year to prepare for, but chances are you'll forget about all that for the time you're in bed
(or wherever) with your partner. The best way to enjoy sex is to forget everything that's going on in the outside world, let go, and just enjoy. But not so
much that you forget the condom.

# What Happens If You Need To Go To The Bathroom While You're Having Sex?

For boys, it's an either-or situation. If his penis is erect, he can't pee. Girls are more likely to feel as if they need to pee during sex with a boy, as the movement of his penis can put pressure on their urethra. A finger can do the same thing if it touches the female prostate (glands on the wall of your vagina). However, that doesn't mean that you will, or even can, pee. Some girls might experience what's known as female ejaculation instead. The liquid that comes out isn't urine, but an odorless fluid from your glands.

Still, if you do find that you really need to go to the bathroom while you're having sex, then taking a quick break should be no problem for two people who are so close. When you're done, just pick right back up where you left off!

# Why Do People Make Love In Bed?

A bed is more than just a great place for a pillow fight. It's comfy, warm and feels secure. Also, sex can tire you out, so if you do it in bed, you can have a snooze afterwards. But you'll probably agree that your bed is a very personal space for you, right? So don't rush things and invite someone in before you're ready. If you do go to bed with someone and then realize that you don't want to be there after all, then pull the emergency brake and get out. Just because you've started something, doesn't mean you have to finish it.

Of course, you don't need to be in bed to make love. You can do it in the bathroom, in a tent, on the beach, in the woods, or in your parents' living room. Trying out different places can be fun and exciting, as long as you don't offend or upset anyone in the process.

# What Is The First Time Like?

Being so physically close to someone for the first time is a very big deal, and most people remember it for the rest of their lives.

When you're thinking about losing your virginity, it's really important that you feel safe and secure with your partner. You need to be able to trust the other person and feel comfortable being naked with him or her. That kind of thing takes time because you have to get to know each other really well first. No one said this was a race. Who cares if your friends have already had sex and are boasting about it? This isn't about them—it's about the two of you. Don't you think it would be a shame to rush your first time, just so you can keep up with everyone else?

Once you do feel ready, relax, try to have fun, and don't expect too much. Have you ever done anything that worked perfectly first time? If you're a boy, it might be that you come really fast because you feel nervous or unsure of yourself. Or you might suddenly lose your erection. Girls, don't worry if you don't have an orgasm the first time around. For a woman to come, both partners have to be really relaxed and it usually takes a bit of practice to find out what works and what doesn't.

As nerve-wracking as your first time might be, the times that come afterwards usually just keep getting better and better. Once you work out what feels good for each other, you can make the most of it and, if you like, start trying out new things. A bit of variety can be pretty exciting.

One last thing—whether you're in a girl-boy, girl-girl or boy-boy situation, talk to each other afterwards, tell each other how it was for you and how you're feeling now.

# Am I Allowed To Watch Porn Online Or On My Phone?

You know how fantasy movies are all mythical heroes, magic swords, glittering fairies, non-stop action, and … er, nothing like reality at all? Well, porn movies aren't that different. It's just that, with them, the women caked in makeup have gigantic breasts and perfectly formed vulvas, and the men caked in makeup have enormous penises. Oh, and then there's the exaggerated "passion", pretend orgasms, and fake semen.

Watching porn won't kill you. Some grown-ups watch it because it turns them on. But if you're young, porn can look scary, make you feel sick, and even cause nightmares. It also risks giving you a distorted idea of sex. Because they can be so disturbing, pornographic images might get lodged in your brain and you could automatically start comparing your own experiences to those you've seen on screen. Or, if you haven't had any sexual experiences yet, you could think that porn is a realistic portrayal of what sex should be like. Adults worry that if children and teenagers are exposed to porn, they won't be able to explore their own sexuality with the freedom and independence they need to really get to know themselves. That's why, in the United States, it is a federal offense for anyone to show porn to a minor, whether it's on DVD, online or anywhere else.

If you have already watched porn and found that it made you feel bad, talk about it with a person you trust. Whether you were forced to watch it, saw it accidentally, or deliberately accessed it, and whether it was commercial porn with actors or "homemade" porn with real people, talking always helps you to deal with things that upset you or make you feel uncomfortable.

# PORN — BASICALLY JUST MAKE-BELIEVE

# How Many Times Is It Okay To Masturbate In A Week?

No idea. Seriously. You're the one who gets to decide how often you masturbate. And if anyone tries to tell you that it's unhealthy, dangerous, or something that only boys do, then they don't know what they are talking about. Masturbating is great. It releases happiness hormones (endorphins) that make you feel great and can even relieve stress. You also get to know your own body better and can explore what works for you and what doesn't. That comes in handy when you feel ready to be with someone else, because you can show them how to turn you on. It's also perfectly fine if you only masturbate occasionally, or even never. Work out what makes you happy, and then go with it!

# On A Scale Of One To Ten, How Much Does It Hurt The First Time You Have Sex?

It's really not all that bad. Most people find that it doesn't hurt at all. A lot of girls have a very stretchy hymen, if they have sex with a boy. Even if they do feel a slight pressure or a short pricking sensation, it will usually pass very quickly. Boys are also very sensitive around their erogenous zones, so whether you're a boy or a girl, you both need to be especially gentle and take care not to hurt each other.

Girls, if things still feel uncomfortable after penetration, it's probably got nothing to do with your hymen. Most likely your vagina is tensing up as if to say, "Nope, not happening!" That's often because of external factors. Maybe you don't feel relaxed or you're both pressed for time? Are you worried that you'll be disturbed? Is everything okay in the contraception department? Probably the most important question to ask here, and in any situation where the sex just isn't working, is whether you both actually want to sleep together. If you have any doubts at all, then hold off and wait a while. Don't put yourselves under pressure by rushing it.

# Boys' Penises Get Hard, But What Happens With Girls?

Pretty much the same thing! You just can't see it from the outside so well because it happens to the clitoris, which is tiny compared to a boy's equipment. When a girl feels all tingly and really turned on, more blood circulates to her vulva and that causes her clitoris to swell and get hard, just like a penis. Her vagina will also become wet. Girls—if none of those things happen, and boys—if you don't get an erection, then you probably aren't aroused and don't want to have sex. Listen to your body and take things at your own pace. That said, some people take longer to get turned on than others, and some girls find that their vagina doesn't get that wet, even though they do want to have sex. If this is the case, there are special lubricants that you can use that work with condoms.

# Do All Girls Bleed The First Time?

No. Lots of girls don't bleed at all, some bleed a little and some bleed a bit more. The blood comes from your hymen breaking and although it's usually just a few drops at most, it can look like more when it mixes with vaginal fluid. Basically, every girl is different because no two hymens are alike. Yours might be really stretchy or it might be really thin. Sometimes the opening in the hymen is quite big, but it can also be quite small. It's even possible to break your hymen while you are playing sports without noticing! There's also a chance it won't break until the second, third, or fourth time you have sex. And some girls don't even have a hymen.

# I Heard Sex Is The Best Thing In The World. Is That True?

Bonobo apes probably think so. They have sex about every 90 minutes. But for them it's not just about satisfying their lust; they also use it to settle disputes and strengthen their sense of connection to each other. Amazing.

As for us humans, we're all free to decide what we think the best things in the world are. For a lot of people, finding a caring relationship with another person is top of the list because it fulfills several desires at once—the desire for someone you can rely on, the desire to share your life experiences, the desire for companionship and, of course, the desire for sex. Most people agree that sex is best when they know the other person, can trust them, and love them deeply.

Your thoughts on what the best thing in life is will also change depending on your age. An average 18-year-old will probably think the freedom to make his or her own decisions is pretty great. Other people might value their friends more than anything else, or their parents for always being there and supporting them. When you're older, you might love your job or be totally absorbed in your children because they fulfill you and make you happy. Hobbies and religious beliefs could also take up a big part of your life.

Sex can be important, for sure, but it's probably best to think of it as just one of life's many joys.

# What Is An Orgasm?

An orgasm happens when you reach the peak of sexual arousal and tension. It's explosive, euphoric, and can make your whole body tingle and shudder. The feeling is created by rhythmic contractions in the muscles and glands of your sex organs. The intense pleasure you get with an orgasm soon subsides into a warm glow that spreads throughout your whole body.

Everyone is capable of having orgasms, but we all differ in the way we get there. When girls masturbate, they usually reach orgasm by stroking or rubbing their clitoris. Boys often hold the shaft of their penis and move their hand up and down. If you're having sex with another person, it can take a little while to learn what they like and how they want to be touched.

# Can You Live Without Sex?

Yes. About one percent of the adult population describe themselves as asexual. They simply have no desire to have sex with anyone else and sometimes find it hard to understand why other people do. Some asexual people will masturbate from time to time, but that's all. Although they're fine with not being sexually attracted to others, society can often make them feel like it's a problem and like there's something wrong with them. Just think about it, sex and passion are two of the most popular ingredients in any film or TV show, and the topics regularly show up in magazines, at school, and in sex-education books, like this one. Anyone who admits to finding the idea of sex boring or even disgusting will soon find themselves the outsider. Nevertheless, more and more asexual people are openly admitting to enjoying and embracing life without sex.

Strong religious beliefs are another reason why people might avoid having sex. Some stay celibate for a short time, others for longer. Also, if one partner dies, it can take the other partner a long time to work through their grief and feel ready to be together with someone new.

Whatever a person's reasons for not having sex, it certainly doesn't mean they have to be lonely.

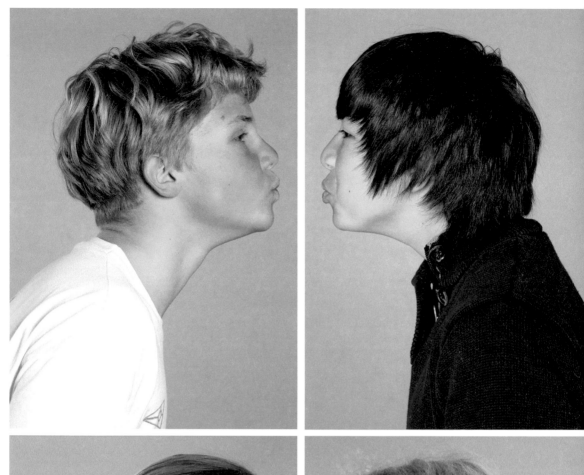

# What Makes You Gay Or Lesbian?

Some researchers believe that a person's sexual orientation begins in the womb—that as a fetus develops, something happens that "decides" whether it will be attracted to men or women later in life. That may or may not be true, but one thing is for sure—we have no control over our own or anyone else's sexual orientation. It can, however, change over time, maybe more than once or maybe very slowly. Some people know where they're headed very early on, while others only work it out further down the line. A lot of people have to wait till the end of puberty before they get an idea of who they are attracted to.

Did you know that dolphins, seals, lions, and hundreds of other species are known to live from time to time, or even their whole lives, with a member of the same sex? Seeing as humans are animals too, why should we be any different? No one can tell you who to love. It's up to you, and you alone. Also, if you figure out that you're lesbian or gay, you're the one who gets to decide who to tell and when. Letting your friends and family know that you are attracted to the same sex is called "coming out".

Also, you might find that you like a boy for a while, and then later get a crush on a girl. That's totally fine. Don't rush into labelling yourself. Just because you've been together with someone of the same sex once, doesn't mean that you're gay, lesbian, or bisexual. Lots of girls feel attracted to other girls during puberty, and some try out kissing each other to see what it's like. Boys can also feel drawn to other boys during puberty, and even if they go for girls later in life, it's not unusual for them to have had their first sexual experience with a boy.

Oh, and your behavior doesn't decide your sexuality. So, boys? If you're someone who's gentle and caring with his friends, that's great! Being like that doesn't automatically mean you're gay. The idea of "manly" men who are always cool and want to have sex all the time is definitely not an image you have to conform to. Women don't have to act typically "feminine" either. Not every girl loves to gossip and not every girl is as sweet as pie. Stereotypes are dull. It's much more interesting if you work out who you are and share it with the world. Just try and develop a thick skin for any idiots who feel like they have something stupid to say about it.

# Is It True That Women Can't Get AIDS?

Gender has nothing to do with it. Whether you're male or female, if you have unprotected sex you risk contracting HIV/AIDS. The virus is passed on when the semen, vaginal fluid, or blood of an infected person gets into another person. Women can become infected if semen carrying the virus comes into contact with the mucous membrane of her vulva or vagina. It can also be passed on through anal sex between two men or a man and a woman. You are at risk if you come into contact with infected blood, including menstrual blood. Oral sex, where semen or vaginal fluid gets into your mouth, carries a small risk of infection. So stay safe and always use a condom.

# Do I Have To Have The Vaccination For Cervical Cancer? Will It Stop Me From Getting Cancer?

Unfortunately, no one has discovered a surefire way to keep people from getting cancer yet. The vaccination we're talking about here just reduces the likelihood of a woman developing cervical cancer. It works by targeting the human papilloma virus (HPV), which is actually a whole family of viruses. Some are known to trigger cervical cancer, but the vaccine doesn't protect against all of them.

About 80 percent of men and women who are sexually active will become infected with HPV at least once in their lives. Sometimes the body's immune system gets rid of the virus itself. In cases where it doesn't, the person might not have contracted the kind of HPV that triggers cancer, but they could still have the kind that will make genital warts appear on their vulva, anus, or penis. The warts don't hurt, but they're unpleasant and you need a lot of treatment to get rid of them.

Because of all this, the Centers for Disease Control recommends that all boys and girls between the ages of 11 and 12 get the vaccine. The current vaccine protects against four types of HPV: the two that are most likely to cause cervical cancer, and the two that are most commonly associated with genital warts. The vaccine involves having three injections in your arm over the course of six months. It's best if it happens before you have sex for the first time. But even if you've already lost your virginity, it can still make sense to get protected, as you might not be infected yet or have only contracted one of the four HPV types. Talk to your parents and reach a joint decision about whether the vaccine is right for you. Condoms do reduce the risk of becoming infected with HPV, but the viruses can also exist outside the genitals, around the pubic area, and can be transmitted by touching.

Whether you choose to go for the vaccine or not, it's still important to visit your OBGYN for regular cervical screening tests once you get older. As we said above, the shots don't remove the risk of cancer altogether, and HPV isn't the only way that cervical cancer can develop.

# ON GETTING PREGNANT ...

# ... AND HAVING BABIES

# WHAT DO YOU DO IF YOU GET PREGNANT
# HOW DO BABIES DEVELOP?

## Why Can't Men Have Babies?

Because they're missing all the equipment. They've got no womb, so there's nowhere for the fertilized egg to live while it grows into a baby. They've got no vagina, so there's no way for the baby to get out when it's ready to be born. And even though men do have nipples, they're no good at producing milk. Bad luck, boys. Earthworms have a better setup. They're hermaphrodites, which means they have both male and female sex organs. A worm can either fertilize another worm or have the babies itself.

# Why Does A Baby Need Nine Months In The Womb?

Yeah, why not 20 or more, like an African elephant? Well, a baby elephant weighs about 220 pounds when it's born, and human babies are a lot lighter than that (thank goodness).

These days, people often say pregnancy actually lasts 10 months because it's impossible to pinpoint the exact day that the egg was fertilized by a sperm. Even though it usually happens around the middle of the woman's menstrual cycle, it's normal to start counting from the first day of her last period.

Nine or 10 months might sound like a long time, but it's actually incredibly short when you consider everything that happens during pregnancy. Once the egg has been fertilized, it takes just three months for the microscopic bundle of cells to grow into a tiny little person. The heart usually starts beating in the fifth week, and by the 12th week all the organs are in place and you can see the arms and legs. From here on in, all the fetus has to do is grow enough so that it can survive in the outside world. If it was born now, it would be in trouble because its lungs aren't properly developed and its skin is paper-thin. However, sometimes things do go a bit wrong and a baby is born far too early. But thanks to advances in modern medicine, babies who arrive in the sixth or seventh month still have a very good chance of survival.

# How Old Does A Girl Have To Be Before She Can Get Pregnant?

Once a girl has her first period, it usually means she is sexually mature and can therefore get pregnant. Ovulation can sometimes take a while to settle into a rhythm, though there's no way of knowing whether or not this is the case. And even if you haven't gotten your period yet, there's still a chance you could get pregnant if you happen to have sex just as your ovaries release their first egg. So whether you've started your periods or not, you should always use a condom. And before it even gets that far, think hard about whether you really feel ready for sex.

# Will Your Eggs Run Out At Some Point?

Most experts would say that when a baby girl comes into the world, her ovaries contain all the eggs she will ever have. A newborn is thought to carry about a million of them. That number will have fallen to roughly 300,000 by the time she reaches puberty. Once she gets her first period, up to 20 eggs will mature each month and the one or two that develop best will be released into a fallopian tube and travel down into the womb. About 400 or 500 eggs ripen between the time a girl gets her first period and the time she reaches menopause, which is when her eggs are all used up. Menopause usually happens around the age of 50.

However, some recent research suggests that women's ovaries actually contain stem cells that can develop into new eggs. The proof is far from conclusive, though, and even in the studies that claimed to find stem cells, it wasn't clear whether or not the new eggs could be fertilized.

Incidentally, you can do your existing eggs a favor by living a healthy life. If you exercise regularly and don't smoke or drink, your eggs will stay fresher for longer.

# Can You Get Pregnant From Masturbating Or From Swallowing Semen?

Masturbation is a really great method of contraception. The only way to get pregnant is if sperm comes into contact with an egg, and one of those two crucial ingredients is missing when you have sex with yourself. You can't get pregnant by swallowing semen either because sperm have to swim up your vagina to reach the egg. That can only happen when you have unprotected sex with a boy, or if he ejaculates close to your vulva and the sperm comes into contact with it. The best thing to do if semen gets onto your upper thighs, or his hands or yours, is to take a break, wash it all off, and then pick up where you left off (with a condom).

# Why Do Men Ejaculate Millions Of Sperm? Does It Have To Be So Many?

Yes. The route leading from a woman's vagina to the egg in one of her fallopian tubes is so full of obstacles that hardly any sperm make it all the way. First, they have to get past the mucus membrane inside a woman's vulva. It's not exactly keen on having guests and the immune cells here see the sperm as enemies and start fighting them off. Further on, lots of sperm end up stuck to thick mucus that closes off the cervix if ovulation hasn't happened yet. The ones that survive will wait it out and continue their journey once the mucus becomes thinner and the cervix opens. But even then, they're still not home free. Deadends are hiding everywhere, and even if they do make it across the womb, there's only one egg waiting for them in the fallopian tube … but which fallopian tube? In the end, just 500 sperm or so reach their goal, and even then a lot of them are too exhausted to even think about fertilizing the egg. The sperm that does manage it should really get a gold medal!

# What Should You Do If You Find Out You're Pregnant?

First, try to stay calm. Visit your doctor or a clinic, like Planned Parenthood, as soon as possible for a test to see if you really are pregnant. If the result is positive, then you'll need some time to think. Getting pregnant by accident when you're a teenager can be very scary. It also feels strange because you're still just a kid yourself—you like messing around, hanging out with friends, and sleeping all day. The last thing you feel ready to do is look after a baby. But in fact most girls who become teenage mothers do manage it, as they find a lot of strength from the child and from their love for it. There are many organizations, like Planned Parenthood or even your local church, that can give you the emotional support you need and also help you to find out what financial options are available if you get pregnant before you are ready. They can also help you with continuing your education and discuss housing options if you are not able to stay at home. Services like Medicaid and WIC (Women, Infants, Children) are available through the government to help cover the cost of medical and living expenses for young mothers. Your doctor or clinic will help you get in contact with the right people. They will also talk to you or offer you counseling services if you are unsure about whether to have the baby or whether to end the pregnancy by having an abortion. Each state has very different laws about if, when, and how you may be allowed to end your pregnancy with an abortion. It is important to know the law in your state and to only seek an abortion in a licensed facility with knowledgeable health care professionals, even if that means that you must travel outside your state. No matter what anyone tells you, it is never a good idea to try any alternative type of abortion, such as herbal, at home, or "back alley" abortions. Not only do these types of abortions put your future ability to have children at risk, they can also put your own life at risk too. Many states also have laws restricting how far into pregnancy you are allowed to have an abortion, so it is important not to wait too long to tell anyone so that all your options will be available. Your local Planned Parenthood clinic is a good resource for information about your reproductive rights.

Even if it does cause some shouting matches at home, it's usually a good idea to let your parents know what's going on. Hopefully they will support you in whatever you decide to do. If you don't feel safe talking to your parents, find another adult that you can trust, such a relative, teacher, or member of your church, to help you figure out what the right decision is for you.

# What Do You Do If Your Girlfriend Gets Pregnant?

Ideally, you don't leave her to deal with it alone. After all, it's your baby as well as hers. You might panic at first because you don't feel ready to have a child. Or maybe you'll get really angry because the condom didn't work or there never was a condom. But the bottom line is that if you love your girlfriend, you should support her. Dealing with a difficult situation alone is much harder than when there's two of you. And even if you aren't together anymore, you still need to be fair to your ex. If you both decide to have the baby, then it's important that you support the mother and help her look after the baby when it arrives. Being part of a pregnancy is a huge step and you'll probably feel like you need help to sort your head out. Talk to your friends or a grown-up who you trust. You can also visit your doctor or a clinic and speak to someone there, either on your own or with your girlfriend or ex.

# What Should You Do If You Get Pregnant But Don't Want To Tell Your Parents?

Talking to friends or a grown-up who you trust is a good way to start, but you also need to speak to your doctor or health care provider as soon as you can. Even if you don't want to tell your parents, in some states the doctor may be required to notify them if you are pregnant or seeking an abortion and they can even require your parents' permission before you are allowed to have an abortion, depending on how old you are. They would probably talk to you about this first, though. If you do decide to tell your parents that you're pregnant, neither they nor anyone else can make you have an abortion.

As a general rule, taking the plunge and telling your parents is often better than carrying such a big secret around with you.

# What Kind Of Pain Is It When You Give Birth?

It's completely different to any kind of pain you might have experienced so far. Have you ever had a filling in your tooth without anesthesia? If you have, you'll know that the pain appears in the blink of an eye, but is also over pretty quickly. When a woman goes into labor, though, the pain builds up gradually as the muscles of her uterus start tensing up and then relaxing, over and over. These tense-and-relax cycles are known as contractions. They come in waves and get stronger and more painful as she gets closer to giving birth. Prenatal classes teach special breathing techniques that help women cope with the contractions. Position and movement can make things easier, too. Kneeling, standing, leaning forward, or walking around are all good things to try out. Also, the knowledge that labor is going to end in a beautiful baby boy or girl means most mothers-to-be can keep going. However, if things get really bad, hospitals can provide injections that will numb the pain.

Even though giving birth hurts a lot, most women find that when they get to hold their baby for the first time, they're so proud and in love that they forget everything that happened before.

# Who Or What Decides Whether A Baby Will Be A Boy Or A Girl?

It all comes down to chromosomes. Most men have an X chromosome and a Y chromosome, while most women have two Xs. That means an egg will always carry an X chromosome, while a sperm cell will carry either an X or a Y. So, a baby's sex depends on the gold-medal sperm that fertilizes the egg. If it's an X sperm, the baby will be a girl. If it's a Y, then a baby boy's on the way. The difference becomes noticeable about eight to 10 weeks into a pregnancy when an XY fetus starts producing the testosterone that will make it develop a penis and testicles. Doctors can identify the sex on an ultrasound image at about 12 weeks—unless the baby decides to cross its legs during the scan!

That said, it can sometimes be hard to tell what sex the baby is, even after the birth. We all differ in height, in the way we look, and in a million other ways besides. It's no different with our sex. Some people, for example, have only one sex chromosome while others have more than two. Also, a person might realize at some point in life that he or she is in the wrong body. It could be that a girl feels strongly that she should be a boy, or vice versa. Nature is a complex thing and its decisions often aren't as black and white as we think.

# Do Babies Fart In The Womb?

If they did, their moms would puff up like balloons and go floating off into the sunset. So it's lucky for us that babies can only pass gas once they're born. When they start breastfeeding or drinking from a bottle, babies often swallow mouthfuls of air along with the milk. Also, the milk can cause gas to form in the digestive system. All that air has to get out somehow, and that's when a tiny toot happens.

But even though there's no farting in the womb, pregnant women still get treated to all kinds of other strange sensations, and you can see a lot of them from the outside. Unborn babies can get hiccups, for example. When that happens, you'll be able to see its mom's belly pulsing along with them. And if the baby gets a burst of energy and starts kicking or boxing in the womb, the sight of all those bumps and lumps appearing and disappearing can be really funny. Sometimes you can tell if it's a hand or foot, but often it's just an unidentifiable limb pushing up into mom's belly and keeping everyone entertained.

# So What Comes After Puberty?

Life just carries on. You might have lots of new experiences, or it might not feel that different from before. Puberty is a natural process that doesn't happen from one day to the next. A lot of people don't even notice it after a while, and then suddenly it's over and they're adults. That doesn't mean everything will stay the same from here on in, though. As you get older, you'll find you have to make new transitions and face new challenges. Starting a job or a career is a big step, as is finding a partner who you might want to settle down with. Also, you can try out crazy new things and discover new sides of yourself at any age. Change is part of life, not just puberty.

# USEFUL LINKS

If you've still got questions or need help of any kind, try checking out these websites. Most of them offer a helpline and/or things like text, web chat and e-mail services.

## GENERAL WEBSITES FOR YOUNG PEOPLE

### www.teenlineonline.org
Teen Line is a confidential, toll-free telephone helpline for teenagers. You can speak with other teenagers who are specially trained to listen and understand your feelings. You can reach them by calling (800)-852-8336, texting "TEEN" to 839863, or by going on their website message board.

### www.thursdayschild.org
Thursday's Child is a toll-free helpline for young people who need advice, advocacy, or just someone to listen. You can reach a counselor by phone 24/7 at (800) usa-kids (872-5437) or you can log on to the website for live support by Skype or e-mail.

### www.youthline.us
YouthLine is a part of the Kristen Brooks Hope Center and can be reached toll-free at (800) YOUTH LINE (968-8454). They offer peer-to-peer counselling on anything from relationships, stress, and grief to STIs, teen pregnancy, and abuse.

## TATTOOS, PIERCING, AND BODY ART

### www.aaatattoodirectory.com
The AAA Tattoo Directory is a directory of shops, artists, conventions, and state regulations to help you choose a safe, reputable parlor for your body art.

### www.safe-tattoos.com
The Alliance of Professional Tattooists, Inc. is a nonprofit organization that offers advice and education on body art. Through their website, they offer information about how to find a safe, reputable tattoo parlor as well as services in your area.

## RELATIONSHIPS, SEX AND CONTRACEPTION

### www.plannedparenthood.org/info-for-teens/
The Planned Parenthood Federation of America is a national organization that provides reproductive health care, information, and advocacy for women

around the country. You can contact Planned Parenthood at (800) 230-PLAN (230-7526) to find a clinic in your area. Their website also offers live chat if you need information and advice right away.

**www.nationalfamilyplanning.org**
The National Family Planning & Reproductive Health Association is a nonprofit organization that works to ensure family planning and reproductive health care services for everyone. Through the NFPRHA website, you can find information on reproductive health care and your rights, such as abortion, contraceptive coverage, sex education, and STIs, as well as links to the over 4600 clinics that they represent nationwide.

**www.ashasexualhealth.org**
The American Sexual Health Association is a nonprofit organization that promotes sexual health and education. On their website, you will find links to resources in your area along with videos and information about your body and sexual health.

**www.guttmacher.org/statecenter/spibs/index.html**
Guttmacher Institute - overview of State policies in brief

**www.positive.org/**
Coalition for positive sexuality (in English and Spanish)

## PREGNANCY
**www.childbirthconnection.org**
Childbirth Connection is a nonprofit organization that helps guide pregnant women and their families through every aspect of childbirth, from prenatal care through birth. On their website, you will find information and resources to help you maintain your health, choose a health care provider, learn about different treatments and tests, and prepare for birth.

**www.prochoice.org**
The National Abortion Federation is an association of abortion providers who can give you honest, unbiased information about what your options are if you get pregnant, including abortion, adoption, or having a baby. You can find links to reproductive services in your area on their website or you can reach a NAF provider at (800) 772-9100. Check with the Abortion Hotline (1-800-772-9100 or www.prochoice.org) for info on restrictions in your state.

**www.abortioncarenetwork.org/mom-dad**
Mom, Dad I'm Pregnant helps young people and their parents communicate effectively. In English and Spanish

**www.ourbodiesourselves.org**
Women's health information and resource center

**www.ourbodiesourselves.org/book/links.asp?topicID=17**
Girls' and young women's health web links

## LESBIAN, GAY, BISEXUAL AND TRANSGENDER (LGBT)

**www.itgetsbetter.org**
The It Gets Better Project offers confidential support and information to the LGBT community and to anyone who is considering issues having to do with their sexuality. It Gets Better includes legal advocacy for LGBT issues, as well as e-mail support and a helpline at (888) 246-PRIDE (246-7743).

**www.thetrevorproject.org**
The Trevor Project offers services to LGBT youth through a social networking community that puts LGBT teens in touch with friends and allies in a safe and accepting environment. The Trevor Project also offers support on their website via text, web chat, and a 24/7 hotline at (866) 488-7386.

**www.fortytonone.org**
The Forty to None project supports young LGBT people who find themselves homeless or living in a hostile environment by helping you to find a safe place to stay in your area and offering counseling and advice by phone and web chat.

## VIOLENCE, SEXUAL ABUSE AND OTHER CRISES

**www.loveisrespect.org**
Love is Respect, in partnership with The National Dating Abuse Hotline, offers advice and education about healthy relationships. If you find yourself in an abusive relationship or know someone who is, Love is Respect has a 24/7 helpline at (866) 331-9474 or you can chat with a peer counselor via text or web chat."

**www.thehotline.org**
The National Domestic Violence Hotline offers support and crisis intervention 24/7 to help victims of abuse find safety. You can reach the hotline toll-free at (800) 799-Safe (799-7233).

**www.boystown.org**
Boys Town can help teens and young people in abusive and unhealthy situations by helping to find a place to stay, counseling, advice, or just someone to listen. Boys Town offers a chat feature on their website, e-mail, in person, or a 24/7 helpline at (800) 448-3000.

# AUTHORS

**Jan von Holleben** was born in 1977. He studied special education in Freiburg before traveling to the UK, where he earned a degree in the theory and history of photography at the Surrey Institute of Art and Design in Farnham. After spending seven years in London as an art director, picture editor, and founder of various art and photography organizations, he returned to Germany and now lives in Berlin.

Jan works for a number of German publications, including *Geo, Geolino, Die Zeit, Zeit Leo, Spiegel, Dein Spiegel, Neon, Eltern, Chrismon* and *SZ Magazin*. When he teamed up with the amazing group of kids and professionals who were involved in *Does this Happen to Everyone?,* he fulfilled a long-held dream: to make a book about puberty that respects its subject matter but isn't afraid to have fun along the way.

**Antje Helms** was born in 1974. She holds an masters in cultural studies and graduated from the Henri Nannen journalism school in 2004. Antje now works as a freelance journalist and concept developer. In 2008, she developed the outline for *Dein Spiegel,* a news magazine aimed at young readers and published by the Spiegel Verlag.

Antje mainly writes on topics to do with family, travel and science. Her clients include German publications and websites such as *ELTERN, stern.de, GeoWissen* and *natur.*

Antje lives in Hamburg with her husband and two daughters.

# IMPRINT

Does This Happen to Everyone?
A Budding Adult's Guide to Puberty

Idea, concept, and photography by
Jan von Holleben
Text by Antje Helms
Translation from German by Jen Metcalf
Adaptation for the U.S. version by Jen Horan

Additional layout by Hendrik Hellige
and Pepita Köhler

Published by Little Gestalten,
Berlin 2014

ISBN: 978-3-89955-521-9
Typefaces: Universe by Adrian Frutiger,
Block Gothic by Steve Jackaman

Printed by Livonia Print, Riga
Made in Europe

The German original edition
*Kriegen das eigentlich alle?* was published
by Gabriel Verlag.
© for the German original: Gabriel Verlag
(Thienemann Verlag GmbH) Stuttgart/Vienna,
2013
© for the English edition: Little Gestalten, an
imprint of
Die Gestalten Verlag GmbH & Co. KG,
Berlin 2014

With support from the Berlin Family Planning
Centre – BALANCE, www.fpz-berlin.de

Bibliographic information published by the
Deutsche Nationalbibliothek.
The Deutsche Nationalbibliothek lists this pub-
lication in the Deutsche Nationalbibliografie;
detailed bibliographic data are available online
at http://dnb.d-nb.de.

This book was printed on paper certified by
the FSC®.

Gestalten is a climate-neutral company.
We collaborate with the non-profit carbon off-
set provider myclimate (www.myclimate.org)
to neutralize the company's carbon footprint
produced through our worldwide business
activities by investing in projects
that reduce $CO_2$ emissions
(www.gestalten.com/myclimate).